# Leadership Is Everyone's Business

**WHETHER ONE-TO-ONE OR ONE-TO-MANY, MOBILIZING OTHERS TO WANT TO WORK TOWARD SHARED ASPIRATIONS IS WHAT LEADERSHIP IS ALL ABOUT.**

It takes solid, trust-based relationships among people—from the shop floor to the executive suite—to get extraordinary things done in organizations. Regardless of rank or position, title or tenure, there is a need for everyone to take the initiative, to inspire others to dream, to help the collective achieve more than what is possible alone.

Most importantly, leadership is available to more than an elite few. For anyone with a desire to make a difference, there are plenty of opportunities to learn, live, and share what it means to be an effective leader—in good times and bad, in start-ups and multi-nationals, whether for-profit or not-for-profit. And for nearly three decades, thousands of aspiring leaders have begun their journey right here, with The Five Practices of Exemplary Leadership®.

# ① Model the Way

To effectively model the behavior they expect from others, leaders must first be clear about their guiding principles. They must *clarify values*. Leaders find their own voices, and then they clearly and distinctively give voice to their values. They set the standard for living those values with integrity. Exemplary leaders know that it's their *behavior* that earns real respect. They practice what they preach. Their words and deeds are consistently aligned. The truth is that you either lead by example or you don't lead at all. Eloquent speeches about common values may inspire for the moment but are not enough to build and sustain credibility—the foundation of leadership and the most important personal quality people look for and admire in a leader.

In simple daily acts, effective leaders set an example for others as they *Model the Way*—from the stories they tell, the way they allocate their time, and the language they use to the recognitions, rewards, and measurement tools they choose. In putting this essential practice into action, leaders build commitment by affirming and communicating shared values that all can embrace and engaging others in achieving common goals.

"If you want to lead others . . . you have to open up your heart. You have to be able to be honest with yourself in order to be honest with others."

**NEVZAT MERT TOPCU**
ENTREPRENEUR MAGAZINE PUBLISHER, TURKEY

# ② Inspire a Shared Vision

Without willing followers, there can be no leaders. And *Inspire a Shared Vision* is the practice that sets leaders apart from other credible people. Leaders engage others in tying their personal dreams to the aspirations of the group to create a shared vision. Only then will these followers commit their talents, time, and energy to working together to achieve greatness.

Passion to make a difference drives leaders to gaze across the horizon of time and imagine the unique opportunities in store when they and their constituents arrive at a distant destination. With no signposts or road maps, exemplary leaders boldly and creatively communicate their hopes and dreams, and together with their teams' desires, forge a unity of purpose that pulls everyone forward with a shared sense of destiny.

By envisioning a future of ennobling possibilities and enlisting others by appealing to shared aspirations leaders *Inspire a Shared Vision*. Leaders breathe life into visions, through vivid language and an expressive style, and uplift others with their infectious enthusiasm and excitement to strive toward achieving the group's goals for the greater good.

Hervé Houdré, general manager and regional vice president of Intercontinental Hotels is a champion of "sustainable hospitality" —a vision of the hotel industry as environmentally forward-looking. Under his leadership, the Willard Hotel in Washington, D.C, won many "green" awards, and he now brings those same principles and practices to New York's InterContinental–The Barclay Hotel.

# ③ Challenge the Process

Great leaders are great learners. And challenge is the crucible for greatness. Exemplary leaders are pioneers at taking the initiative in searching for innovative ways to improve their own work, that of their teams, and their organizations. Rejecting the status quo, they experiment and take risks, treating the inevitable mistakes as important learning opportunities and creating a safe environment in which others can learn from failures as well as from successes. Always open to new opportunities that test their abilities, leaders know that innovation comes more from listening than from telling. They "get out of the box" as they actively seek out and recognize good ideas—from anyone, from anywhere— and take the lead in challenging the system to adopt those products, processes, services, or systems that improve the way things get done. Exemplary leaders also create a climate in which others feel safe and supported in taking risks and stepping outside their comfort zones.

The work of leaders is change, and making a commitment to *Challenge the Process* requires a willingness to take action, every day: to look outward for innovative ways to improve, to experiment and take risks, to constantly generate small wins—making it easy for the team to succeed in making progress—and to continually learn from experience.

Jeff Orton, CIO and chief logistics officer at Genesco in Nashville, Tennessee, helped break down the "silos" of multiple departmental agendas by challenging the organization to change their way of thinking and work together toward the common goal of focusing on the customer.

# ④ Enable Others to Act

Exemplary leaders know they can't do it alone. Leadership is a team effort, not a solo expedition. And only solid trust and strong relationships can transform shared visions into reality. Helping others to see themselves as capable and powerful—to nurture positive self-esteem—is key to mastering the art of mobilizing others in joining the journey toward a common destination. When leaders involve others in decision making and goal setting, and build teams with spirit, cohesion, and a true sense of community, they make it possible for teamwork, trust, and empowerment to flourish. Leaders strengthen everyone's capacity with shared goals and shared roles that bind people together in collaborative pursuits.

Leaders make sure that when they win, everybody wins. They share power and information as well as, build the capabilities and capacities of others to be successful. Leaders act as coaches and teachers, giving people challenging tasks, clearing away obstacles, and supporting others with the tools they need to be successful. By fostering collaboration, building trust, and facilitating relationships, leaders *Enable Others to Act* with increased self-determination and competence.

> **"I need to give power to other people, allowing them the creativity and freedom to explore new ideas and ways of thinking."**

**JILL CLEVELAND**
FINANCE MANAGER, APPLE, INC.

# ⑤ Encourage the Heart

When striving for excellence, especially in time of great change, people can become physically and emotionally exhausted. They can become frustrated and disenchanted. They often are tempted to give up. Exemplary leaders know that getting extraordinary things done in organizations is hard work, and yet they rise to the call to inspire others with courage and hope. When striving to raise quality, recover from disaster, start up a new service, or make dramatic change of any kind, leaders make sure that people understand in their hearts that what they do matters. They expect the best, share the spotlight and credit for a job well done, celebrating people's accomplishments in personal and meaningful ways.

Leaders *Encourage the Heart* by putting into action the principles and essential practices that support our basic human need to be appreciated for who we are and for what we do. In big ways and small—from marching bands and T-shirts to simple and heartfelt thank-yous—leaders recognize contributions by showing appreciation for individual excellence and celebrate the values and victories by creating a spirit of community.

"Everybody wants to feel that they matter. You can get a lot accomplished by making other people feel important."

**MANISH CHANDRA**
SIEBEL SYSTEMS

# Profiles in Leadership

## TRUE TO THE ADAGE THAT THE MORE THINGS CHANGE, THE MORE THEY STAY THE SAME . . .

While the context of leadership may have changed over nearly three decades of study, the content of leadership has remained virtually the same. What constituents and followers look for today in their leaders remains as consistent and defined as it was in the early 1980s when we first began inquiring into what ordinary people do to get extraordinary things done in organizations.

Dispelling the myth that leadership is the exclusive purview of a select few, over the years we have given voice to thousands of everyday people, in every line of work, in every industry—from individual contributors to front-line managers, administrative professionals to community service volunteers—whose personal stories demonstrate that leadership is available to all who choose to accept the challenge. Regardless of title or privilege, leaders are enthusiastic participants in change. They try, fail, and learn from their mistakes. They build self-confidence by learning from others and about themselves, capitalizing on their strengths and overcoming weaknesses. They understand that leaders go first, that the legacy they leave is the life they lead. And, most importantly, just as anyone would to perfect his or her golf game or master the violin, leaders practice, practice, practice.

## LEADERS MAKE A DIFFERENCE

The question is not will you make a difference but, rather, what difference will you make. Leadership is an aspiration and a choice. And exemplary leaders choose to put leadership into practice, every day in every way, to achieve extraordinary results and to facilitate the development of the leadership capacity in all those who choose to follow.

As decades of research has proven—and thousands of leadership case studies reveal—every individual has within him or her the capacity to lead . . . and to make a difference.

# Tom Johnson

**CHIEF EXECUTIVE OFFICER, AÉROPOSTALE, INC**

**HEADQUARTERS:** Midtown Manhattan

**EMPLOYEES:** 14,000

**BUSINESS:** A mall-based specialty retailer of casual apparel and accessories for pre-teens and young adults, operating over 1,000 stores across the U.S. and Puerto Rico and Canada.

> **"**We don't just sell t-shirts. We inspire others to be the best that they can be.**"**

Creating a culture driven to please the ever-changing fashion tastes of today's pre-teen and young adults may seem daunting. Yet Aéropostale has achieved both record-setting business growth and recognition as "One of the Top 40 Companies to Work for in New York"—an honor that draws much-deserved attention to the company's vision of being one of the finest corporate cultures in all of retail.

Continuous building on the company's brand momentum, particularly in the hyper-competitive retail industry, calls for something unique: an aspect of quality and value delivered to the customer unavailable anywhere else. That something "special" is what Aéropostale is all about.

Tom Johnson leads one of the nation's hippest and trendiest clothing retailers for young people, 14 to 17 years old, and pre-teens ages 7 to 12. First launched as a store within clothing retail giant R. H. Macy & Company in 1987, Aéropostale has branched out across the country and internationally to fulfill its mission of becoming *the* dominant, promotional specialty store in the teen retail space. And one thing Tom Johnson knows for sure: it is only by partnering with Aéropostale's 14,000+ employees that the company's mission can be fully realized.

Going far beyond just paying lip service to the adage that "people are a company's greatest asset," Tom is dedicated to nurturing and growing a developed culture that puts employees and customers first—one that is open and honest, that thrives on communication and celebration, and that honors the contributions of everyone, at every level, throughout the organization. And that success begins with the hiring process, according to Tom, who believes that "hiring right" is key to perpetuating the four core values that drive the Aéropostale culture: teamwork, integrity, compassion, and respect.

According to Sean Morrison, vice president, Learning and Development, "People sense they can make a difference and that they contribute to the success of the company. Whether you work in the corporate office, on merchandising or design, or in the stores, every day there is a measure of success." And in his own personal experience with Tom's leadership, Sean added, "He's given me projects I've never done before, but I felt really confident in doing them because he had confidence in me."

While today there are daily celebrations and collaboration, a common language about goals and aspirations, and solid teamwork that provides support and encouragement to everyone—from the stockroom to sales associates to senior management—it wasn't always that way.

"In the very early days of my leadership," Tom admits, "I realized that not everybody had the same drive, or thought process, or passion toward the end goal that I might have." Being open to feedback and insight provided by others, Tom learned that he needed to take more time and listen, to really find out what was important to the people who worked with him as teammates.

Today Tom acknowledges that "it's better to cross the finish line with all of your teammates, rather than crossing the finish line all by yourself. And that's how we operate." Open and available, Tom is seen by others as a great example of someone who recognizes everyone's individual contributions and supports the efforts of all to be their best.

"There's not a day, in my 20 years, when I haven't wanted to come to work here," Julie Sedlock, group vice president, Operations observed. "That's crazy! I talk to my contemporaries and friends, and no one has a situation like this. And it's not just my job, it's this place! When you create this community where people really feel valued, that your opinion will be heard . . . you want to come to work, you want to try harder, you want to get to the goals we've set for the organization."

In life and in business, Tom lives by a few very simple mottos: first love yourself and then believe that you can impact both your own life and the lives of others—insight into the most fundamental principle of leadership that he may have acquired from his father.

As a young man, when Tom asked his brick-layer father what he did, his dad's inspiring answer was, "I build cities." With this transformative notion of how every individual plays a critical role in creating something bigger and grander than oneself, Tom has gone on to cultivate a model of leadership at Aéropostale for others who want to build and sustain a truly unique and profitable brand to follow.

# Jennifer Ernst

**DIRECTOR, BUSINESS DEVELOPMENT, PALO ALTO RESEARCH CENTER (PARC)**

**HEADQUARTERS:** Palo Alto, CA

**EMPLOYEES:** 250 multi-discipline professionals, 80 percent with doctoral degrees

**BUSINESS:** A commercial center for innovation that works with clients worldwide to successfully bring leading-edge research and innovation to market

**"Play to the strengths of your organization and play to the strengths of your people."**

In the heart of Silicon Valley lies an internationally renowned research hub destined to continue its legacy of defining the future of technology. When first created as the R&D arm of Xerox Corporation in 1970, the assembled group of multi-disciplinary, world-class researchers became known as Xerox PARC. Tasked with the lofty goal of creating "The Office of the Future," over the next 30+ years the team made its mark. Under the sheltering umbrella of its parent company, Xerox PARC produced such breakthrough innovations as computer programming languages, laser printing, and Ethernet networking to fiber optics and biomedical systems.

Soon after 2002, however, when PARC was incorporated as a wholly owned yet independent subsidiary company of Xerox, the challenges of change and transformation truly began. A full-fledged business entity, solely in charge of ensuring its own financially sustainable future, PARC Inc. embarked on a transformative path to corporate independence and profitability.

Once confident and sure of exactly who they were, what they did, and what products they produced, nothing could be counted on anymore. As Jennifer Ernst, director of business development observed, "We made a major change. And that means ground rules had to go out the window. Everything at PARC that you assumed to be true may or may not be and had to be called back into question."

PARC was undergoing a fundamental shift in organizational structure: moving from a funding model as a research lab to a revenue model as a commercial growth engine. Where Xerox was once PARC's singular client, the new organization faced the difficult challenge of having to play in a competitive marketplace for business and sales. And yet, while its researchers excelled at thinking through the early stages of product development, the organizational mindset was not attuned to thinking about all of the various steps required to get that product to market.

At the center of this change, Jennifer saw opportunity to help successfully transition PARC from where it had been to where it needed to be. Working as a bridge between researchers and clients, she listened carefully for unexpressed assumptions, often hearing not only what people said, but also what they didn't. And as she set out to help everyone learn how to do things differently, to think in different ways, Jennifer relied on creativity and ingenuity to get her message out—to make her case for what she believed in, for her vision.

Presenting test cases and innovative exercises to the senior team was one approach that Jennifer used to great affect, challenging them to define and plan for a future that answered the most fundamental business questions: Who are we? What do we sell? and What do we want our future to look like when we grow up? At one off-site, for example, Jennifer presented each small group with a short bio-sketch of an individual customer and a single white box—empty except for an array of markers, pencils, paints, and other art supplies needed to create a design for a product.

"That white box represented what our future needed to be," CEO Mark Bernstein recalls with a smile. "And it was up to us to fill it up. But the distance between where we found ourselves— shaking the boxes and making jokes about what we *were* selling—and the realization that that was the task at hand . . . it was a shock."

Praised for her ability to elevate what is good for PARC above her own personal agenda establishes a level of credibility fundamental to Jennifer's success. "She knows that she has to make a difference in order for PARC to be successful," added Bernstein. "And she willingly accepts that commitment with a whole lot of vigor and a sense of purpose."

"There are no magic answers for going through a transformation," says Jennifer. "You do have to be honest in painting a picture of where you want to get to and where you're starting from. And that goes down to the individual level with individual people."

"So know where you're headed. Allow people to help shape that direction. Play to the strengths of your organization and play to the strengths of your people. Then be honest about what pieces you're going to have to change."

# Learning to Lead

Wanting to lead and believing that you can are the departure points on the path to leadership development. No matter where you are on your leadership journey, improvement is always possible. You can be a better leader than you are today. You can be more effective. You can make more of a positive difference than you are making now—in your organization, at home, in the community, in the world.

Extraordinary things aren't done in huge leaps forward. They are done one step at a time. And if practice makes perfect, nowhere does that ring more true than in leadership development. Noting that real change begins when we turn our workplaces into practice fields for leadership, we provide solid evidence that shows why deliberate practice, as part of an ongoing leadership development process, is critical to becoming the best leader you can be.

**"Leadership opportunities are presented to everyone . . . what makes the difference between being a leader and not is how you respond in the moment."**

**MICHELE GOINS**
SENIOR VP AND CHIEF INFORMATION OFFICER FOR JUNIPER NETWORKS

# The Leadership Challenge Story

Created by James M. Kouzes and Barry Z. Posner in the early 1980s and first identified in their internationally best-selling book, *The Leadership Challenge*, The Five Practices of Exemplary Leadership® approaches leadership as a measurable, learnable, and teachable set of behaviors.

After conducting hundreds of interviews, reviewing thousands of cases studies, and analyzing more than one million survey questionnaires to understand those times when leaders performed at their personal best, there emerged five practices common to extraordinary leadership achievements.

Now, nearly 30 years later and with data from over three million leaders around the world, this eminently practical model of leadership development has stood the test of time, continuing to prove its effectiveness in cultivating and liberating the leadership potential in any person—at any level, in any organization—who chooses to accept the challenge to lead.

## EVIDENCE-BASED TOOLS FOR DEVELOPING LEADERS

Self-discovery and self-awareness are critical to developing the capacity to lead. And personal reflection and analysis of one's own leadership behaviors are core components in that process. Equally as valuable is insight from those who know individual leaders well, who have experience of them in a leadership role, and who are committed to supporting the leader's personal development and willing to provide honest feedback. The Leadership Practices Inventory (LPI) instrument, initially developed to validate the findings of our original Personal Best Leadership case studies, is an essential tool to help leaders gain perspective into how they see themselves as leaders, how others view them, and what actions they can take to improve their effectiveness.

The LPI-Self assessment, for example, offers individual leaders a way of independently measuring their own leadership behaviors, while the LPI-Observer gathers important 360-degree insight from bosses, co-workers, direct reports, and others who have direct experience of the individual in a leadership role. These 30-item instruments measure the frequency of specific leadership behaviors on a 10-point scale, with responses to six behavioral statements for each of The Five Practices. It does not evaluate IQ, leadership style, or management skill. Rather, leaders and observers indicate how frequently the leader engages in the important behaviors associated with The Five Practices that research has demonstrated, year after year, make for more effective leaders.

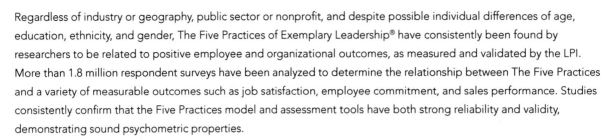

## ACROSS BORDERS, CULTURES, AND GENERATIONS

Regardless of industry or geography, public sector or nonprofit, and despite possible individual differences of age, education, ethnicity, and gender, The Five Practices of Exemplary Leadership® have consistently been found by researchers to be related to positive employee and organizational outcomes, as measured and validated by the LPI. More than 1.8 million respondent surveys have been analyzed to determine the relationship between The Five Practices and a variety of measurable outcomes such as job satisfaction, employee commitment, and sales performance. Studies consistently confirm that the Five Practices model and assessment tools have both strong reliability and validity, demonstrating sound psychometric properties.

**Today, ongoing empirical research continues to reaffirm that leaders who engage in The Five Practices are more effective and successful than those who do not, and are perceived by others as:**

- Having a high degree of personal credibility
- Effective in meeting job-related demands
- Able to increase motivation levels
- Successful in representing the group or team to upper management
- Having a high-performance team
- Fostering loyalty and commitment
- Reducing absenteeism, turnover, and stress levels

**In addition, those working with exemplary leaders are shown to feel more committed, powerful, and influential. Significantly more satisfied with their leader's practices and strategies, they also are more likely to:**

- Be proud to tell others they're part of the organization
- Feel a strong sense of team spirit
- See their own personal values as consistent with those of the organization
- Feel attached and committed to the organization
- Have a sense of ownership of the organization

For the most current research, abstracts, and other important information about the Leadership Practices Inventory and The Five Practices of Exemplary Leadership®, visit **www.leadershipchallenge.com/go/research**.

# About the Authors

James M. Kouzes and Barry Z. Posner are preeminent researchers, award-winning writers, and highly sought-after teachers in the field of leadership. Jim is Dean's Executive Professor of Leadership, Leavey School of Business, Santa Clara University. Barry is Professor of Leadership at Santa Clara University where he served as dean of the Leavey School of Business for 12 years (1997–2009).

In books and workbooks, training materials and workshops, assessments and videos, Jim and Barry have been writing on leadership for nearly 30 years, examining leaders, leadership, and leadership development from several points of view. Together, they are authors of the award-winning *The Leadership Challenge* (over 1.8 million copies sold) plus other best-selling books that include *The Truth About Leadership*, *A Leader's Legacy*, *Credibility*, *Encouraging the Heart*, *The Leadership Challenge Workbook*, and *The Leadership Journal*. They also developed the highly acclaimed *Leadership Practices Inventory (LPI)*, a 360-degree assessment tool and The Leadership Challenge® Workshop, both based on The Five Practices of Exemplary Leadership® model.

For more information about Jim or Barry—to contact them, view their speaking schedule and full biographies, or find out more about the entire library of leadership knowledge and tools they have authored—visit **www.leadershipchallenge.com**.

# THE FIVE PRACTICES AND TEN COMMITMENTS OF EXEMPLARY LEADERSHIP®

## 1 MODEL THE WAY

**1**. Clarify values by finding your voice and affirming shared ideals.

**2**. Set the example by aligning actions with shared values.

## 2 INSPIRE A SHARED VISION

**3**. Envision the future by imagining exciting and ennobling possibilities.

**4**. Enlist others in a common vision by appealing to shared aspirations.

## 3 CHALLENGE THE PROCESS

**5**. Search for opportunities by seizing the initiative and by looking outward for innovative ways to improve.

**6**. Experiment and take risks by constantly generating small wins and learning from experience.

## 4 ENABLE OTHERS TO ACT

**7**. Foster collaboration by building trust and facilitating relationships.

**8**. Strengthen others by increasing self-determination and developing competence.

## 5 ENCOURAGE THE HEART

**9**. Recognize contributions by showing appreciation for individual excellence.

**10**. Celebrate the values and victories by creating a spirit of community.

## A Leadership Challenge Resource

© 2011 by James M. Kouzes and Barry Z. Posner.
Published by The Leadership Challenge®, A Wiley Brand.
All Rights Reserved.

DISCOVER MORE AT:

**WWW.LEADERSHIPCHALLENGE.COM**

# Notes

# Notes

# Notes

# Notes

# Notes

# Notes

# Notes

# Notes

# Notes

# Notes

# Notes

# Notes